THE GREAT PHILOSOPHERS

Consulting Editors
Ray Monk and Frederic Raphael

LOCKE

Michael Ayers

ROUTLEDGE
New York

2054890

Published in 1999 by
Routledge
29 West 35th Street
New York, NY 10001

First published in 1997 by
Phoenix
A Division of the Orion Publishing Group Ltd.
Orion House
5 Upper Saint Martin's Lane
London WC2H 9EA

10 9 8 7 6 5 4 3 2 1

Library of Congress Cataloging-in-Publication Data

Ayers, Michael, 1935–
        Locke / Michael Ayers.
          p. cm.—(The great philosophers : 8)
        Includes bibliographical references.
        ISBN 0-415-92383-2 (pbk.)
        1. Locke, John, 1632–1704. Essay concerning
        human understanding—Criticism and interpretation.
        I. Title. II. Series: Great Philosophers (Routledge
        (Firm)) : 8.
B1294.A94 1999
192—dc21   99-22647
                                                          CIP

To Delia

LOCKE

Ideas and Things

INTRODUCTION

John Locke lived from 1632 until 1704, a period of political and intellectual turmoil and transformation in Europe, not least in England. From his mid-thirties, when he left Oxford to join the household of the first earl of Shaftesbury, founder of the Whig party, Locke was at the heart of it. He became a friend of leading scientists, among them 'the father of chemistry' Robert Boyle, the pre-eminent physician Thomas Sydenham and the greatest of them all, Isaac Newton. He collaborated with Sydenham in particular, and himself practised as a medical doctor. He briefly held government office when Shaftesbury was in power under Charles II, but later wrote and, very probably, plotted against both Charles and his brother James II. He travelled in France in the 1670s, meeting scientists and philosophers. In 1683, after the Rye House plot to assassinate Charles and James, he went into exile in Holland, there completing three major, still canonical works. *A Letter on Toleration* and *Two Treatises of Government* addressed the two great political issues of the time, religious toleration and constitutional government. His most important work, however, *An Essay concerning Human Understanding*, was in general philosophy. After returning to England on James's deposition, he continued to write extensively on philosophy and religion until his death, but these interests did not absorb all his considerable energies. He gave economic advice to the government, and held the important post

3

of Secretary to the Board of Trade and Colonies from 1696 to 1700.

In metaphysics and epistemology Locke fought on two main fronts. Scholastic Aristotelianism, if intellectually a spent force in the last decades of the seventeenth century, still had influence and a voice, and the *Essay* supplied detailed alternative theory – in effect, an alternative university textbook. More importantly, together with Newton's *Principia* the arguments of the *Essay* effectively decided the issue in the battle between 'gods' and 'giants'. These adversaries, now known as 'Rationalists' and 'Empiricists', were, on one side, those proponents of the new mechanistic approach to physics, chiefly Cartesians, who adopted a broadly Neoplatonist epistemology, seeing knowledge in terms of a match between human and divine ideas; and, on the other side, those who fitted the new physics into a less theological, more sense-based and naturalistic theory of knowledge, and were mainly influenced by the Epicurean, Pierre Gassendi. During the first twenty or thirty years of the eighteenth century, the *Essay* and *Principia* gradually shaded out their Cartesian rivals, and it was in their shade that the next great philosophical movement, idealism, gradually acquired its form and strength.

Perhaps no modern philosopher, unless Kant, has had a wider influence than Locke, and Kant was himself deeply indebted to his celebrated predecessor. Yet Locke has not had a good press in the twentieth century, and the historic importance of his philosophy may be surprising to someone who first dips into the *Essay* and finds, perhaps, its rambling, repetitive, figurative, disputatious style, its rhetoric and heavy irony unworthy of a famously powerful philosophical intellect. Even academic philosophers, it seems, have had difficulty getting beneath the surface imprecision of Locke's writing to the sinewy, radical theses propounded. But Locke wrote for his time and for a readership he understood. Although we may regret it, it is hardly appropriate to criticize the style of that unusual achievement, an influential best-seller in metaphysics which remained so for well over a century. It may now be hard work to read, but the *Essay*'s reputation is reviving. Philosophers are beginning to relearn how it was capable of changing the direction of European thought, and to find in it, for all that is time-bound or problematic, still pertinent lessons for ourselves.

Whether a broadly Lockean, if revised and corrected, undogmatic realism is preferable to some form of broadly Kantian, if modified and updated, idealism remains a living philosophical question – perhaps the central metaphysical question of our time. This little book, however, will attempt only to expound and explain some elements of Locke's extended argument against dogmatic philosophies of science, embodying his view of the relation between experience and theory. What is discussed is selected out of a ramified, systematic and wide-ranging philosophy, a philosophy which helped to determine what counts as philosophy in modern European culture.

IDEAS AND THINGS

A key concept of Locke's, as of much philosophy of his time, is that of an 'idea'. Ideas are what the mind is 'employed about whilst thinking'. They constitute the content of thought, content variously expressible by nouns, adjectives and verbs: that is, words that can stand as subjects or predicates. In one sense 'ideas' are concepts, or ways of conceiving of things, but they are also objects of thought, 'concepts' in the old-fashioned sense of 'things as conceived of', or aspects of things as picked out in thought. Locke's primary epistemological thesis is that the ways in which we conceive of the world, including ourselves, are determined by the ways in which we experience the world. There are no innate ideas, and there is no innate grasp of the way the world ultimately is:

> 2. Let us then suppose the mind to be, as we say, white paper, void of all characters, without any *ideas*; How comes it to be furnished? Whence comes it by that vast store, which the busy and boundless fancy of man has painted on it, with an almost endless variety? Whence has it all the materials of reason and knowledge? To this I answer, in one word, from *experience*: in that, all our knowledge is founded; and from that it ultimately derives itself. Our observation employ'd either about *external, sensible objects; or about the internal operations of our minds, perceived and reflected on by*

ourselves, is that, which supplies our understandings with all the materials of thinking. These two are the fountains of knowledge, from whence all the ideas we have, or can naturally have, do spring. (*An Essay concerning Human Understanding*, II.i.2)

Locke's claim here is directly opposed to a famous argument of Descartes, that the various sensations caused by a piece of melting wax require interpretation by the intellect, employing the innate, non-sensory idea of matter, before they constitute experience of a substantial, enduring stuff undergoing change. Another important difference from Descartes lies in Locke's conception of our awareness of the 'operations of our minds', which he calls 'reflection'. Traditionally, in Aristotelian as well as Cartesian philosophy, the mind's reflexive awareness of its own activity, taken to supply concepts of different kinds of thought, is a function of intellect, not sense. Indeed, for Cartesians it is through reflexive self-awareness that we can achieve explicit access to such innate, intellectual ideas as those of substance, duration, thought and even (through reflection on our own imperfection) the positive idea of perfection, or God. For Locke, in contrast, 'reflection' is simply a part of 'experience': 'though it be not sense, as having nothing to do with external objects; yet it is very like it, and might properly enough be call'd internal sense' (II.i.4). An important implication is that thought is not, as Descartes had held, transparent to itself. Just as the senses give us only superficial, coarse knowledge of external objects, so 'reflection' keeps us aware of our thinking, but not of the ultimate nature of thought.

The thesis that all our ideas *ultimately* derive from experience unpacks as the claim that every idea is either directly given in experience or somehow constructed from given ideas. Hence Locke's distinction between simple and complex ideas. Yet his account of simple ideas involves certain difficulties:

> 1. ... Though the qualities that affect our senses, are, in the things themselves, so united and blended, that there is no separation, no distance between them; yet 'tis plain, the ideas they produce in the mind, enter by the senses simple and unmixed. For though the sight and touch often take in from the same object, at the same time, different ideas; as a man sees at once motion and colour; the hand feels softness and warmth in the same piece of wax: yet the simple ideas thus united in the same subject, are as perfectly distinct, as those that come in by different senses. The coldness and hardness, which a man feels in a piece of ice, being as distinct ideas in the mind, as the smell and whiteness of a lily; or as the taste of sugar, and smell of a rose: and there is nothing can be plainer to a man, than the clear and distinct perception he has of those simple ideas; which being each in itself uncompounded, contains in it nothing by one uniform appearance, or conception in the mind, and is not distinguishable into different ideas.

> 2. ... When the understanding is once stored with these simple ideas, it has the power to repeat, compare, and unite them even to an almost infinite variety, and so can make at pleasure new complex ideas. (II.ii.1–2)

For Locke, an object appears to possess a variety of distinct sensible qualities, not because the perceived qualities are really distinct entities in the object (where they are, on the contrary, 'united and blended'), but just because of the variety of ways in which the object acts on us through the senses. Qualities are *aspects* of things, marked off from one another only by the different ways we have of perceiving things. One might object that, plausible as this claim may be with respect to the distinction between a lily's smell and its whiteness, or even between the hardness and coldness of ice, the conceptual distinction between, for example, a thing's shape and its motion, or its shape and its colour, is not due to a primitive or given articulation of sensory appearance. A pink patch does not *appear* as a duality of shape and colour, however natural it may be to abstract one from the other. There is, then, from its first introduction, something problematic about Locke's conception of given simple ideas. Occasionally – for example, when considering the question of which ideas of extension are simple – Locke himself confesses, somewhat truculently, that the compositional, simple–complex model fits some cases only approximately: 'It is enough for Mr Locke that his meaning can be understood. It is very common to observe intelligible discourses spoiled by too much subtilty in nice division'. (Fifth edition, II.xv.9, footnote) His meaning, no doubt, is that any ideas not themselves given in experience must be constructed by *some* sort of extrapolation from ideas so given, even if they are not straightforwardly *composed* of such ideas.

PRIMARY AND SECONDARY QUALITIES, POWERS AND SENSITIVE KNOWLEDGE

It is neither the precise form of Locke's constructivism nor its tenability which will be pursued here, but arguments in which he develops the notion of a difference between the way something is in itself and the way in which we ordinarily conceive of it. The following sections are preliminary to his famous distinction between primary and secondary qualities:

> 7. To discover the nature of our ideas the better, and to discourse of them intelligibly, it will be convenient to distinguish them, as they are ideas or perceptions in our minds; and as they are modifications of matter in the bodies that cause such perceptions in us: that so we *may not* think (as perhaps usually is done) that they are exactly the images and *resemblances* of something inherent in the subject; most of those of sensation being in the mind no more the likeness of something existing without us, than the names, that stand for them, are the likeness of our ideas, which yet upon hearing they are apt to excite in us.

> 8. Whatsoever the mind perceives in itself, or is the immediate object of perception, thought, or under-standing, that I call *idea*; and the power to produce any idea in our mind, I call *quality* of the subject wherein that power is. Thus a snowball having the power to

produce in us the ideas of *white, cold,* and *round,* the
powers to produce those ideas in us, as they are in the
snowball, I call *qualities;* and as they are sensations, or
perceptions, in our understandings, I call them *ideas:*
which ideas, if I speak of sometimes, as in the things
themselves, I would be understood to mean those
qualities in the objects which produce them in us.
(II.viii.7–8)

Despite these explanations, the terminology employed in
the ensuing discussion is notoriously slippery. The distinc-
tions drawn here between sensory ideas and the 'modifications of matter' causally responsible for those ideas, and
between the powers of bodies to produce ideas and the
ideas produced, are not firmly maintained. For example,
Locke here proposes to call certain powers, as they are in
bodies ('as they are in the snowball'), 'qualities'; and to call
them, as they are experienced ('as they are sensations, or
perceptions, in our understandings'), 'ideas'. That makes
the 'idea', in effect, a way the object appears to us, and the
'quality' the power of the object to appear that way. Yet
traditional usage of the expressions 'in the object' and 'in
the mind (understanding)' made it possible to say that the
idea is the quality as it is in (i.e. appears to) the mind, and
the quality is the idea as it is in the object. Consequently, as
his next sentence concedes, Locke uses 'quality' and 'idea'
(or 'simple idea') virtually interchangeably, failing to
adhere to his own proposal.

Moreover, the 'power' or 'quality' in the object is not
something distinct from, or over and above, the 'modification of matter' (i.e. the intrinsic property of the material

object) in virtue of which the object appears in that particular way. Locke spells this out in direct discussion of the idea of *power* itself. He attributes the idea of power to experience of regular patterns of change – experience which gives rise, first, to expectations that 'like changes will for the future be made in the same things, by like agents, and by the like ways', and then to the thought that in one thing there exists the possibility of being changed and in another, 'the possibility of making that change'. So we form the idea of *power*, active and passive: the power of fire to melt wax and the power of wax to be melted are aspects of fire and wax known and identified only through their joint effect. The idea of a power to X is thus an indirect conception of an attribute of which X-ing is the observable sign, an attribute which could in principle be directly known. Thus we can refer in thought, if indirectly, to that unknown attribute. All this explains how – to anticipate the next passage – Locke can assert that 'what is sweet, blue, or warm in idea [i.e. in appearance, 'in the mind'], is nothing but the bulk, figure, and motion of the insensible parts in the bodies themselves, which we call so'.

Complaints about Locke's relaxed use of his own terminology are common, but his practice only matches the slipperiness of ordinary ways of talking about appearance and the objects of perception and thought. For example, if I short-sightedly see an H on my optician's chart as an N, there is point in asserting, but also point in denying, that the N existing only 'in my mind' *is* the H 'in the object', misperceived. Neither assertion nor denial of the identity is 'right' as opposed to the other. No doubt Locke felt it enough 'if his meaning can be understood'. One way of expressing his meaning in the next passage is to say that some properties that we take ourselves to perceive in things are intrinsic to them, while others are relative to perception – no *more* than powers to appear a certain way in virtue of otherwise imperceptible intrinsic properties:

9. Qualities thus considered in bodies are, first such as are utterly inseparable from the body, in what estate soever it be; such as in all the alterations and changes it suffers, all the force can be used upon it, it constantly keeps; and such as sense constantly finds in every particle of matter, which has bulk enough to be perceived, and the mind finds inseparable from every particle of matter, though less than to make itself singly be perceived by our senses. *v.g.* Take a grain of wheat, divide it into two parts, each part has still *solidity*, *extension*, *figure*, and *mobility*; divide it again, and it retains still the same qualities; and so divide it on, till the parts become insensible, they must retain still each of them all those qualities. For division (which is all that a mill, or pestle, or any other body, does upon another, in reducing it to insensible parts) can never take away either solidity, extension, figure, or mobility from any body, but only makes two, or more distinct separate masses of matter, of that which was but one before, all which distinct masses, reckon'd as so many distinct bodies, after division make a certain number. These I call *original* or *primary qualities* of body, which I think we may observe to produce simple ideas in us, *viz.* solidity, extension, figure, motion, or rest, and number.

10. Secondly, such *qualities*, which in truth are nothing

in the objects themselves, but powers to produce various sensations in us by their *primary qualities*, i.e. by the bulk, figure, texture and motion of their insensible parts, as colours, sounds, tastes, *etc.* These I call *secondary qualities*. To these might be added a third sort which are allowed to be barely powers though they are as much real qualities in the subject, as those which I to comply with the common way of speaking call *qualities*, but for distinction *secondary qualities*. For the power in fire to produce a new colour, or consistency in wax or clay by its primary qualities, is as much a quality in fire, as the power it has to produce in me a new idea or sensation of warmth or burning, which I felt not before, by the same primary qualities, *viz.* The bulk, texture, and motion of its insensible parts. (II.viii.9–10)

Here Locke is, in effect, promoting his preferred version of the 'New Philosophy' or 'New Science': that is, the view, dominant by the end of the seventeenth century, that the physical world is ultimately intelligible as a vast machine composed of a uniform matter forming tiny 'corpuscles' (roughly, the atomic theory, although not all 'corpuscularians' accepted indivisible atoms). In so far as these sections constitute an argument for, rather than bare assertion of, mechanistic corpuscularianism, it is, first, that simply to experience or conceive of an external object or body, it has to be experienced or conceived of as possessing 'primary' qualities. Second, we can understand how the 'insensible parts' of a body, in virtue of their determinate primary qualities, can act on our sense-organs so as to cause sensations of colour and the like. Locke concludes that there is no important difference in status between two sorts of powers a body may have, both due to its corpuscular structure: its powers to cause changes in other bodies, and its powers to cause sensations of secondary qualities in perceivers.

It might be asked why Locke should assume that the power to appear red is not in general simply due to the body's *being* intrinsically red, as the power to appear square is in general, we assume, due to its being square. Alternatively, we might question this last assumption: how can we be sure that the power to appear square is not based on some other, perhaps quite unimaginable property of the object? In some ways the latter question reflects Locke's own approach to the issue, to judge by his general account of the 'sensitive knowledge' we have of the existence of external objects:

> 2. 'Tis therefore the actual receiving of ideas from without, that gives us notice of the *existence* of other things, and makes us know, that something doth exist at that time without us, which causes that idea in us, though perhaps we neither know nor consider how it does it: for it takes not from the certainty of our senses, and the ideas we receive by them, that we know not the manner wherein they are produced: *v.g.* whilst I write this, I have, by the paper affecting my eyes, that idea produced in my mind, which whatever object causes, I call *white*; by which I know, that that quality or accident (*i.e.* whose appearance before my eyes, always causes that idea) doth really exist, and hath a being without me. And of this, the greatest assurance I can possibly

have, and to which my faculties can attain, is the testimony of my eyes, which are the proper and sole judges of this thing ...

3. *The notice we have by our senses, of the existing of things without* us, though it be not altogether so certain, as our intuitive knowledge, or the deductions of our reason, employ'd about the clear abstract ideas of our own minds; yet it is an assurance that *deserves the name of knowledge.* If we persuade ourselves, that our faculties act and inform us right, concerning the existence of those objects that affect them, it cannot pass for an ill-grounded confidence: for I think nobody can, in earnest, be so sceptical, as to be uncertain of the existence of those things which he sees and feels. At least, he that can doubt so far, (whatever he may have with his own thoughts) will never have any controversy with me; since he can never be sure I say anything contrary to his opinion. As to myself, I think GOD has given me assurance enough of the existence of things without me: since by their different application, I can produce in myself both pleasure and pain, which is one great concernment of my present state. This is certain, the confidence that our faculties do not herein deceive us, is the greatest assurance we are capable of, concerning the existence of material beings. For we cannot act anything, but by our faculties; nor talk of knowledge itself, but by the help of those faculties, which are fitted to apprehend even what knowledge is. (IV.xi.2–3)

Locke is here emphatically asserting, against Descartes and others, that the senses themselves deliver knowledge without need for ratification or interpretation by reason or intellect. The senses are basic, independent cognitive faculties, even if the knowledge of the world that they provide is more of practical than theoretical value. Since in sensation we are aware not only of an appearance or 'idea', but that something is acting on us, causing the idea, we are able to characterize or identify this external cause *through* the idea, precisely as whatever regularly causes that idea (Locke here says, too strongly, 'always causes'). So the sensory idea of white serves in thought as a sign of that aspect of things which regularly causes that idea or appearance. My perceptual knowledge that something white exists before me is therefore independent of any hypothesis as to what, in the object, constitutes its being white.

Locke's account of 'sensitive knowledge' does not discriminate between primary and secondary qualities. With respect to our primitive perceptual *knowledge*, it seems, things known to exist are known simply as subjects of powers to cause sensations. Consistently with this proposal, Locke treats the distinction between primary and secondary qualities not as something evident in sense perception itself, but as a reasonable hypothesis about the nature of reality, a piece of 'natural philosophy' which goes beyond sensitive knowledge. What, then, makes the hypothesis reasonable? Seen from this direction, what calls for justification is less the proposal that colours in objects are mere powers to appear in certain ways than the assumption that ideas of primary qualities are *more* than merely causally correspondent to certain unknown attributes of things. Locke's response is his claim that the primary qualities supply our only understanding both of what external objects actually *are* and of what they *do*. The latter gets particular emphasis:

11. The next thing to be consider'd, is how *bodies* produce *ideas* in us, and that is manifestly *by impulse*, the only way which we can conceive bodies operate in.

12. If then external objects be not united to our minds, when they produce ideas in it; and yet we perceive *these original qualities* in such of them as singly fall under our senses, 'tis evident, that some motion must be thence continued by our nerves, or animal spirits, by some parts of our bodies, to the brains or the seat of sensation, there to *produce in our minds the particular ideas we have of them.* And since the extension, figure, number, and motion of bodies of an observable bigness, may be perceived at a distance by the sight, 'tis evident some singly imperceptible bodies must come from them to the eyes, and thereby convey to the brain some *motion*, which produces these ideas, which we have of them in us.

13. After the same manner, that the ideas of these original qualities are produced in us, we may conceive, that the *ideas of secondary qualities* are also *produced, viz. by the operation of insensible particles on our senses.* For it being manifest, that there are bodies, and good store of bodies, each whereof is so small, that we cannot, by any of our senses, discover either their bulk, figure or motion, as is evident in the particles of the air and water, and other extremely smaller than those, perhaps, as much smaller than the particles of air, or

water, as the particles of air or water, are smaller than pease or hail-stones. Let us suppose at present, that the different motions and figures, bulk, and number of such particles, affecting the several organs of our senses, produce in us those different sensations, which we have from the colours and smells of bodies, *v.g.* that a violet, by the impulse of such insensible particles of matter of peculiar figures, and bulks, and in different degrees and modifications of their motions, causes the ideas of the blue colour, and sweet scent of that flower to be produced in our minds. It being no more impossible, to conceive, that God should annex such ideas to such motions, with which they have no similitude; than that he should annex the idea of pain to the motion of a piece of steel dividing our flesh, with which that idea hath no resemblance. (II.viii.11–13)

Locke's position, then, is that the primary qualities are privileged in a broad supposition or hypothesis about external objects which allows us to understand in general terms how they might act on one another and on the organs of sense, ultimately the brain, to give rise to sensory experience. There is no similar reason to regard ideas of secondary qualities as more than bare effects, comparable to the pain dependably caused by certain circumstances:

16. ... Why is whiteness and coldness in snow, and pain not, when it produces the one and the other idea in us; and can do neither, but by the bulk, figure, number and motion of its solid parts? (II.viii.16)

Locke seems to be denying, paradoxically, that snow is

white and cold, and in a way he is. But he is not denying that I can tell by sight when, in an ordinary sense, something white exists before me. He is rather trying, as it were, to peel off the subjective, qualitative character of whiteness from what whiteness is 'in the object', as if it is the former purely visual character that the term 'white' primarily or strictly signifies. His quarrel is less with what we ordinarily *mean* by 'Snow is white' than with the language we employ to express what we mean, which seems to him to embody a popular mistake:

> 2. ... And we are sure [that all our simple ideas] agree to the reality of things. For if sugar produce in us the ideas, which we call whiteness, and sweetness, we are sure there is a power in sugar to produce those ideas in our minds, or else they could not have been produced by it. And so each sensation answering the power, that operates on any of our senses, the idea so produced, is a real idea, (and not a fiction of the mind, which has no power to produce any simple idea;) and cannot but be adequate, since it ought only to answer that power: and so all simple ideas are adequate. 'Tis true, the things producing in us these simple ideas, are but few of them denominated by us, as if they were only the causes of them; but as if those ideas were real beings in them. For though fire be call'd painful to the touch, whereby is signified the power of producing in us the idea of pain; yet it is denominated also light, and hot; as if light and heat, were really something in the fire, more than a power to excite these ideas in us; and therefore are called qualities in, or of the fire. But these being nothing,

in truth, but powers to excite such ideas in us, I must, in that sense, be understood, when I speak of secondary qualities, as being in things; or of their ideas, as being in the objects, that excite them in us. Such ways of speaking, though accommodated to the vulgar notions, without which, one cannot be well understood; yet truly signify nothing, but those powers, which are in things, to excite certain sensations or ideas in us. Since were there no fit organs to receive the impressions fire makes on the sight and touch; nor a mind joined to those organs to receive the ideas of light and heat, by those impressions from the fire, or the sun, there would yet be no more light, or heat in the world, than there would be pain if there were no sensible creature to feel it, though the sun should continue just as it is now, and Mount *Aetna* flame higher than ever it did. Solidity, and extension, and the termination of it, figure, with motion and rest, whereof we have the ideas, would be really in the world as they are, whether there were any sensible being to perceive them, or no: and therefore those we have reason to look on as the real modifications of matter; and such as are the exciting causes of all our various sensations from bodies. (II.xxxi.2)

Note that here Locke departs from his previously recommended use of 'quality' for the power in the object, employing it instead, perhaps more naturally, for the qualitative way in which the object is presented in sense experience. But note too his insistence that, when secondary qualities are ordinarily predicated of things, what the predicates 'truly signify' are powers 'to excite certain sensations or ideas in us': that is, to appear in certain ways. These propositions, in Locke's view, are ordinarily expressed in language which reflects a false assumption, but they are not themselves false. In this way, 'sensitive knowledge' is not impugned.

Locke's position is thus fairly subtle, but it is open to certain objections. In particular, the suggestion seems misconceived that such terms as 'white' and 'sweet', in their primary or proper senses, signify ideas *rather than* being predicable of things. To oppose ideas and things in this way assumes a radical and problematic interpretation of the causal model for representation deployed in Locke's account of sensitive knowledge. For it suggests that an idea is a blank mental effect which the subject can name, for example, 'white' independently of any reference to such external objects or situations as cause that idea: as if only after such private naming can 'white' be predicated of objects in a secondary or loose sense to mean *liable to cause white ideas*, as a painful saddle is one liable to cause pain. But that is to depart from the preferable model, discussed above, which takes an 'idea' to be a way in which something appears or is conceived of – or, to use a traditional formulation, to be something perceived or conceived of, *as* it is perceived or conceived of. Now 'white' is not, in its primary sense, a predicate of blank mental effects, but it *is* a predicate of things *as they appear to sight*, connoting how they appear. Yet if that is what is meant by saying that 'white' in its proper sense signifies an idea, then that is precisely how the term is being used when it is said that sugar is white, and Locke's complaint about language is misconceived. The tension between these two models causes difficulties elsewhere in Locke's philosophy and, indeed, in philosophy after Locke. (Wittgenstein attacks the first model in his famous 'private language' argument.)

There are other problems with Locke's lists of primary and secondary qualities. One is that neither list is conceptually uniform. Whiteness and sweetness are both strongly sense-relative, in that they are conceptually tightly linked to particular ways in which things appear to sight and taste. If there were no such thing as vision, but there were intelligent creatures who, through some non-visual sensitivity to light, could perceptually discriminate just the class of things we discriminate as white, then those creatures would not thereby know what *whiteness* is. As Locke insists, someone blind from birth cannot learn precisely what 'white' and 'red' mean. Heat and light, however, are conceptually different. They are natural states or processes with characteristic appearances, but someone incapable of feeling heat could still well understand what 'hot' means: for example, what is meant by the statement that water boils when heated. The term is semantically linked to the physical reality, rather than to its sensory appearance. That was so even when it was unknown, or less well known than it is now, what heat ultimately is, since heat has always been identifiable through a whole variety of observable effects or manifestations, not just through how it feels.

PRIMARY QUALITIES AND
'THE NEW PHILOSOPHY'

Finally, Locke's list of primary qualities is open to objection. Number seems out of place, in that when many things have a joint effect, it is not their *number* which does the work. Solidity has a questionable status for a contrary reason. Accepting a common analogy between mechanics and geometry, Locke assumed that the actual properties of bodies entail their powers – that is, how they will interact – much as theorems are entailed by the defining properties of geometrical figures. Like Boyle before him, he frequently reminds us how clocks owe their particular capabilities to their actual, perceptible mechanical structure:

> 25. ... I doubt not but if we could discover the figure, size, texture, and motion of the minute constituent parts of any two bodies, we should know without trial several of their operations one upon another, as we do now the properties of a square, or a triangle. Did we know the mechanical affections of the particles of *rhubarb, hemlock, opium,* and a *man,* as a watchmaker does those of a watch, whereby it performs its operations, and of a file which by rubbing on them will alter the figure of any of the wheels, we should be able to tell beforehand, that *rhubarb* will purge, *hemlock* kill, and *opium* make a man sleep; as well as a watchmaker can, that a little piece of

paper laid on the balance, will keep the watch from going, till it be removed; or that some small part of it, being rubb'd by a file, the machine would quite lose its motion, and the watch go no more. The dissolving of silver in *aqua fortis*, and gold in *aqua regia*, and not *vice versa*, would be then, perhaps, no more difficult to know, than it is to a smith to understand, why the turning of one key will open a lock, and not the turning of another. (IV.iii.25)

In broad terms this view had been advocated by Descartes, but with important differences. Descartes rejected the very concept of empty space, holding it evident to reason that the fundamental properties of matter are simply extension and, following from extension, motion and rest geometrically defined. The fundamental law of inertia, from which Descartes purported to deduce all other laws, is upheld by an immutable God as He maintains the world in being. From Locke's opposed point of view, a development of Robert Boyle's, solidity fulfils two roles. First, it is a property of bodies conceptually distinguishing them from empty space; second, it is an actual property underlying the power of bodies to interact mechanically, according to laws following from their own nature as bodies, without recourse to divine agency:

1. The idea of *solidity* we receive by our touch; and it arises from the resistance which we find in body, to the entrance of any other body into the place it possesses, till it has left it. There is no idea, which we receive more constantly from sensation, than *solidity*. Whether we move, or rest, in what posture soever we are, we always

feel something under us, that supports us, and hinders our farther sinking downwards; and the bodies which we daily handle, make us perceive, that whilst they remain between them, they do by an insurmountable force, hinder the approach of the parts of our hands that press them. That which thus hinders the approach of two bodies, when they are moving one towards another, I call *solidity* ... [The word] carries something more of positive in it, than *impenetrability*, which is negative, and is, perhaps, more a consequence of *solidity*, than *solidity* itself ...

2. This is the idea belongs to body, whereby we conceive it *to fill space*. The idea of which filling of space, is, that where we imagine any space taken up by a solid substance, we conceive it so to possess it, that it excludes all other solid substances ...

5. ... *Upon the solidity of bodies* also *depends their mutual impulse, resistance and protrusion* ...

6. If any one asks me, *What this solidity is*, I send him to his senses to inform him ... The simple ideas we have are such, as experience teaches them us; but if beyond that, we endeavour, by words, to make them clearer in the mind, we shall succeed no better, than if we went about to clear up the darkness of a blind man's mind, by talking; and to discourse into him the ideas of light and colours. (II.iv.1–2, 5–6)

Locke's distinction between solidity and the power of impenetrability, and his insistence that solidity is an indefinable sensible quality such that a single sense experience can teach us what it is, accords with his suggestion that his primary qualities constitute what is necessary for any understanding of what bodies fundamentally *are*, and consequently of what they do. 'Solid bodies are impenetrable', it is implied, is an axiom linking an actual, intrinsic property (comparable in status to shape) to a causal property or power. Yet this suggestion is, and always was, untenable. To feel the solidity of an object is not to perceive a simple sensible quality, the nature of which is captured by how it feels, and in virtue of which the object is interacting mechanically with your body – supporting it, pressing into it or whatever. Rather, as Locke's own language might suggest, it is to be tactually aware of such an interaction itself. The qualitative aspect of what it is like to feel something press into you, or keep your hands apart, gives no insight into an intrinsic property of the body responsible for its felt resistance. But that is what would be necessary to satisfy the mechanist ideal of intelligibility, and the programme of reducing powers to actual properties.

However cogent any or all of these objections to Locke's distinction may be, his most general epistemological purpose is not undermined, which was to establish that, in themselves, the objects of sense experience may be very different from the way in which we ordinarily conceive of them on the basis of that experience. That may now seem an obvious truth, but Aristotelians had envisaged no such division as Locke recognized between the level of 'natural history', or observation and experiment, and the level of scientific understanding. They assumed that rational reflection on generalizations based on experience leads naturally to 'science': that is, to systematic knowledge of the functional essences or natures of the different kinds of things, essences in terms of which the properties of things can be explained (as observable properties of a heart, for example, can be explained by its function). Descartes, in contrast, did recognize a sharp division between natural experiential belief and theory about the ultimate nature of things. But Descartes held that pure intellect is innately capable of 'science' – of grasping the principles of mechanistic physics without reference to experience. Accordingly, he had considerably less time and respect for pretheoretical belief or probability than Locke. The Cartesian view was opposed by two commonsensical Lockean principles: first, that the senses themselves supply *knowledge* of our environment, albeit coarse, phenomenal knowledge; and, second, that what lies beyond experience remains the topic of speculation starting from experience, and the subject of at best probable conclusions.

This commonsensical, anti-dogmatic core of Locke's argument may seem overlaid in his main discussion of primary and secondary qualities by a desire to establish the nature of bodies in themselves. He may seem eager simply to replace one scientific conception of matter by another – Descartes' by Boyle's. Yet where Descartes appealed to the alleged power of reason to perceive the essence of matter clearly and distinctly, and therefore infallibly, Locke appealed to what, he judged, made best sense, or any sense at all, to limited human faculties. The 'corpuscularian hypothesis' is simply the one which 'seems to go farthest in an intelligible explication of the qualities of bodies', but it falls a long way short of a clear and secure understanding of natural necessity (IV.iii.16).

SUBSTANCE, ACCIDENT AND DOUBTS ABOUT ESSENCE

The same ambivalent attitude towards mechanistic corpuscularianism runs through Locke's theory of substance, a polemical response to earlier theories which constitutes an important development of the experience–theory distinction. Here is the famous opening of the chapter, 'Of our Complex Ideas of Substances':

1. The mind being, as I have declared, furnished with a great number of the simple ideas, conveyed in by the *senses*, as they are found in exterior things, or by *reflection* on its own operations, takes notice also, that a certain number of these simple ideas go constantly together; which being presumed to belong to one thing, and words being suited to common apprehensions, and made use of for quick dispatch, are called so united in one subject, by one name; which by inadvertency we are apt afterward to talk of and consider as one simple idea, which indeed is a complication of many ideas together; because, as I have said, not imagining how these simple ideas can subsist by themselves, we accustom ourselves, to suppose some *substratum*, wherein they do subsist,

and from which they do result, which therefore we call *substance*.

2. So that if any one will examine himself concerning his *notion of pure substance in general*, he will find he has no other idea of it at all, but only a supposition of he knows not what support of such qualities, which are capable of producing simple ideas in us; which qualities are commonly called accidents. If anyone should be asked, what is the subject wherein colour or weight inheres, he would have nothing to say, but the solid extended parts: and if he were demanded, what is it, that that solidity and extension inhere in, he would not be in a much better case, than the *Indian* before mentioned; who, saying that the world was supported by a great elephant, was asked, what the elephant rested on; to which his answer was, a great tortoise; but being again pressed to know what gave support to the broad-backed tortoise, replied, something, he knew not what. And thus here, as in all other cases, where we use words without having clear and distinct ideas, we talk like children; who, being questioned, what such a thing is, which they know not, readily give this satisfactory answer, that it is *something*; which in truth signifies no more, when so used, either by children or men, but that they know not what; and that the thing they pretend to know, and talk of, is what they have no distinct idea of at all, and so are perfectly ignorant of it, and in the dark. The idea then we have, to which we give the general name substance, being nothing, but the supposed, but unknown support of those qualities, we find existing,

which we imagine cannot subsist, *sine re substante*; without something to support them, we call that support *substantia*; which, according to the true import of the word, is in plain *English, standing under*, or *upholding*. (II.xxiii.1–2)

Locke is evidently raising the question of the relationship between things and their sensible qualities, mentioned above, but there has been much debate as to his precise point. ('Things', it should be said, are here 'substances' in the traditional sense, including substantial objects as well as stuffs.) The key to interpreting section 1 is Locke's accusation that people (i.e., in particular, philosophers) mistakenly suppose that they have simple ideas of substances, when in fact their complex conceptions are composed of a number of ideas of qualities ('simple ideas') such as experience has found to 'go constantly together' in individual cases. Locke's own explications make clear that the 'one name' which misleads people is any general name such as 'horse', 'swan', 'gold' or 'water'. For Aristotelians, a 'simple' definition is one which encapsulates the unitary essence of the kind of thing defined, as 'Man is a rational animal' was supposed to do. The Cartesians held a related view, since for Descartes the essences of his two substances, matter and spirit, are the 'simple natures', extension and thought. Roughly, Locke is saying that none of our definitions or conceptions of kinds of substance takes us beyond a list of observable qualities and powers to the intrinsic underlying nature of the substance responsible for those qualities and powers – to what the substance actually *is*. The very notion of a substance (or *substratum* – a related Aristotelian term) arises because we must suppose something more unitary than the recurrently co-existing, but otherwise disparate observable qualities, something 'from which they do result'.

Once again, then, Locke is distinguishing between things as they appear to observation and things as they are intrinsically. But, whereas in identifying some qualities as primary Locke is postulating how things (in all probability) are in themselves, his account of our ideas of substances is manifestly less optimistic. In section 2, this more sceptical view of corpuscularian theory is spelled out. The 'notion of pure substance in general' is represented, in effect, as a bare place-marker for the unknown unitary essence of any substance, opposed to all its observable qualities ('commonly called accidents', i.e. the Aristotelian term for non-essential attributes). To say that qualities such as colour and weight 'inhere in', and are products of, 'the solid extended parts' of their subject (i.e. to propose the very version of the 'corpuscularian hypothesis' that Locke himself favours) is to leave open the question: what is it that that solidity and extension inhere in? In other words, it is to leave unexplained what makes these parts or particles solid and extended. All we can say is that *something* does so. This problem arises for Locke even with respect to 'primary qualities' precisely in so far as he is dissatisfied with available mechanical theory.

A difficulty on which Locke focuses is that of cohesion. He dismisses contemporary attempts to explain cohesion, whether the cohesion of particles with one another or the internal cohesion of the individual particles. Without an understanding of cohesion, extension itself remains mysterious:

23. If any one says, he knows not what 'tis thinks in him; he means he knows not what the substance is of that thinking thing: no more, say I, knows he what the substance is of that solid thing. Farther, if he says he knows not how he thinks; I answer, neither knows he how he is extended; how the solid parts of body are united, or cohere together to make extension. For though the pressure of the particles of air, may account for the *cohesion of several parts of matter*, that are grosser than the particles of air, and have pores less than the corpuscles of air; yet the weight, or pressure of the air, will not explain, nor can be a cause of the coherence of the particles of air themselves. And if the pressure of the aether, or any subtler matter than the air, may unite, and hold fast together the parts of a particle of air, as well as other bodies; yet it cannot make bonds for itself, and hold together the parts, that make up every the least corpuscle of that *materia subtilis*. So that that hypothesis, how ingeniously soever explained, by shewing, that the parts of sensible bodies are held together, by the pressure of other external insensible bodies, reaches not the parts of the aether itself; and by how much the more evident it proves, that the parts of other bodies are held together by the external pressure of the aether, and can have no other conceivable cause of their cohesion and union, by so much the more it leaves us in the dark, concerning the cohesion of the parts of the corpuscles of the aether itself ...

25. I allow, it is usual for most people to wonder, how anyone should find a difficulty in what they think, they every day observe. Do we not see, will they be ready to say, the parts of bodies stick firmly together? Is there anything more common? And what doubt can there be made of it? And the like, I say, concerning *thinking*, and *voluntary motion*: do we not every moment experiment it in ourselves; and therefore can it be doubted? The matter of fact is clear, I confess; but when we would a little nearer look into it, and consider how it is done, there, I think, we are at a loss. (II.xxiii.23, 25)

Locke's scepticism was directed not against the view, which he shared, that many seemingly qualitative phenomena have mechanical explanations, but against the assumption that such explanations, as currently framed, could supply the last explanatory word. For they themselves presuppose conditions which are left unexplained. Locke's point could be illustrated by his favourite example. In a sense, perhaps, in seeing how the cogs and wheels of a clock are connected, one sees how it *must* work. But that is at best only on the assumption that the cogs are coherent and rigid, not fragile and elastic. As Locke argues, the mere familiarity of coherent objects does not relieve us of the need to explain cohesion, if our aim is full understanding of what is going on. And a mechanical explanation of coherence is circular.

Locke brings various other criticisms against mechanism, from the difficulty of making sense of the infinite divisibility of matter, and the problem of understanding how one body 'borrows' an attribute, motion, from another body

(II.xxiii.28; cf. II.xxi.4), to the less metaphysical problem of understanding the 'original rules [of motion] and communication of motion' (IV.iii.30) – laws which we could suppose ourselves to have identified, for Locke, only if we grasped why they must be as they are. In later writings Locke laid emphasis on gravity, for the inverse square law seemed to him (as to Newton) to be a particularly brute regularity calling for further explanation, lacking the quasi-geometrical 'intelligibility' of some other Newtonian laws. His arguments may raise doubts about the mechanists' ideal of intelligibility itself, but it was an appropriate response to the overconfident dogmatism of Cartesians in particular, to demand to know 'what substance exists that has not something in it, which manifestly baffles our understandings'.

It was also appropriate to frame this healthy scepticism within an argument about 'substance' and 'accidents'. An important feature of both Cartesian theory and the dogmatic empiricism of Hobbes is the pretension to have clarified the metaphysical substance–accident relation, the relation between bodies and their properties. Aristotelian accounts of this relation seem to leave us with a multiplicity of irreducible sensible qualities ('sensible forms') and powers mysteriously contained in the unitary substance. Some Scholastics drew the paradoxical conclusion that accidents are only contingently and naturally dependent on the substances in which they inhere, claiming that God can miraculously maintain sensible qualities in existence without the substance which naturally and normally supports them. This thesis, presupposed in the doctrine of transubstantiation, the orthodox interpretation of the

Eucharist (in which the substance of Christ's flesh and blood was taken to underlie the sensible qualities of bread and wine), was only an extreme form of the view that Locke derided:

> 19. They who first ran into the notion of *accidents*, as a sort of real beings, that needed something to inhere in, were forced to find out the word *substance*, to support them ... And he that enquired, might have taken it for as good an answer from an *Indian* philosopher, that substance, without knowing what it is, is that which supports the earth, as we take it for a sufficient answer, and good doctrine, from our *European* philosophers, that *substance* without knowing what it is, is that which supports *accidents*. So that of *substance*, we have no *idea* of what it is, but only a confused obscure one of what it does. (II.xiii.19)

The 'New Philosophers', on the other hand, claimed to have reduced this phenomenal and conceptual multiplicity to an intelligible unity, removing the mystery from 'inherence'. If bodies are nothing but matter in motion, and qualitative differences between them are simply, in Hobbes's expression, 'a diversity of seeming', then the whole problematic relation of substance to accidents reduces to the simple relation between an extended thing and its shape (i.e. limits) and motion – in Cartesian terms, to the relation between extension and its modes. Since, as Hobbes remarked, everyone understands that relation, the ontological problem disappears. Locke's account of our idea of substance – and, in particular, of our idea of solid, extended substance – was a challenge to such optimism. The New

Philosophy may have made the Aristotelian elephant redundant, but it still had need of its tortoise. What goes for ideas of the Aristotelian species or natural kinds goes for ideas of the types of substance postulated by 'New Philosophers', matter and mind, 'body' and 'spirit':

3. An obscure and relative idea of substance in general being thus made, we come to have the *ideas of particular sorts of substances*, by collecting such combinations of simple ideas, as are by experience and observation of men's senses taken notice of to exist together, and are therefore supposed to flow from the particular internal constitution, or unknown essence of that substance. Thus we come to have the ideas of a man, horse, gold, water, *etc.* of which substances, whether anyone has any other clear idea, farther than of certain simple ideas coexisting together, I appeal to everyone's own experience. 'Tis the ordinary qualities, observable in iron, or a diamond, put together, that make the true complex idea of those substances, which a smith, or a jeweller, commonly knows better than a philosopher; who, whatever substantial forms he may talk of, has no other idea of those substances, than what is framed by a collection of those simple ideas which are to be found in them; only we must take notice, that our complex ideas of substances, besides all these simple ideas they are made up of, have always the confused idea of *something* to which they belong, and in which they subsist: and therefore when we speak of any sort of substance, we say it is a *thing* having such or such qualities, as body is a *thing* that is extended, figured and

capable of motion; a spirit a *thing* capable of thinking; and so hardness, friability, and power to draw iron, we say, are qualities to be found in a loadstone. These and the like fashions of speaking intimate, that the substance is supposed always *something* besides the extension, figure, solidity, motion, thinking, or other observable ideas, though we know not what it is. (II.xxiii.3)

There are other passages in which Locke suggests that certain natural forms of language 'intimate the confession of all mankind' (III.viii.2) that we are ignorant of the underlying essences of substances. But here he picks on the notion of 'things' as the bearers of primitive noun-predicates, in effect on the role of 'substances' (material things and stuffs) as the primitive or fundamental subjects of predication in natural languages. This undoubted and celebrated logical feature of natural language certainly invites philosophical explanation, but Locke's analysis (despite its survival into later philosophy, including Kant's) is hardly tenable. Yet his thesis is not so far from views which are not only tenable, but likely to be true. Among them is the view that material things owe their status as primitive objects of discourse to their being naturally and independently unified individuals, given or picked out as such in pretheoretical sense experience, although the causes of their physical unity, and of their other observable features, may be unknown.

MIND AND MATTER

The thought that the substance is something besides extension, figure, solidity, motion or thinking is, for Locke, the thought that we are ignorant of the nature or essence both of whatever is solid and extended, and of whatever thinks. In the chapter on our ideas of substances, Locke puts the point in terms which seem to presuppose that these are, in fact, two distinct substance-types:

> 5. The same happens concerning the operations of the mind, *viz,* thinking, reasoning, fearing, *etc.,* which we concluding not to subsist of themselves, nor apprehending how they can belong to body, or be produced by it, we are apt to think these the actions of some other substance, which we call *spirit,* whereby yet it is evident, that having no other idea or notion, of matter, but *something* wherein those many sensible qualities, which affect our senses, do subsist; by supposing a substance, wherein *thinking, knowing, doubting,* and a power of moving, *etc.* do subsist, *we have as clear a notion of the substance of spirit, as we have of body;* the one being supposed to be (without knowing what it is) the *substratum* to those simple ideas we have from without; and the other supposed (with a like ignorance of what it is) to be the *substratum* to those operations, which we experiment in ourselves within. 'Tis plain then, that the idea of corporeal *substance* in matter is as remote from

our conceptions, and apprehensions, as that of spiritual *substance*, or *spirit*; and therefore from our not having any notion of the *substance* of spirit, we can no more conclude its non-existence, than we can, for the same reason, deny the existence of body: it being as rational to affirm, there is no body, because we have no clear and distinct idea of the *substance* of matter; as to say, there is no spirit, because we have no clear and distinct idea of the *substance* of a spirit. (II.xxiii.5)

This section introduces an argument against dogmatic materialism which runs throughout the chapter (shaping section 23, for example, quoted above). Yet the argument that we have as clear a conception of spirit as we do of matter, on the grounds that we lack a clear conception of either, is hardly a satisfactory basis for 'even a tentative mind–body dualism. The only positive ground given for dualism is the suggestion that thinking appears to us as a property peculiarly incapable of mechanical explanation, but from Locke's own standpoint that appearance could simply be due to our ignorance of a single essence underlying both thought and mechanical properties. Indeed another passage (which supplies a nice example of Locke's anti-dogmatic rhetoric) spells out just this point:

6. ... We have the *ideas* of *matter* and *thinking*, but possibly shall never be able to know, whether any mere material being thinks, or no; it being impossible for us, by the contemplation of our own *ideas*, without revelation, to discover, whether omnipotency has not given to some systems of matter fitly disposed, a power to perceive and think, or else joined and fixed to matter so

40

disposed, a thinking immaterial substance: it being, in respect of our notions, not much more remote from our comprehension to conceive, that GOD can, if he pleases, superadd to matter a faculty of thinking, than that he should superadd to it another substance, with a faculty of thinking; since we know not wherein thinking consists, nor to what sort of substances the Almighty has been pleased to give that power, which cannot be in any created being, but merely by the good pleasure and bounty of the Creator. For I see no contradiction in it, that the first eternal thinking being should, if he pleased, give to certain systems of created senseless matter, put together as he thinks fit, some degrees of sense, perception, and thought ... What certainty of knowledge can anyone have that some perceptions, such as *v.g.* pleasure and pain, should not be in some bodies themselves, after a certain manner modified and moved, as well as that they should be in an immaterial substance, upon the motion of the parts of body: body as far as we can conceive being able only to strike and affect body; and motion, according to the utmost reach of our ideas, being able to produce nothing but motion, so that when we allow it to produce pleasure or pain, or the idea of colour, or sound, we are fain to quit our reason, go beyond our ideas, and attribute it wholly to the good pleasure of our Maker. For since we must allow he has annexed effects of motion, which we can no way conceive motion able to produce, what reason have we to conclude, that he could not order them as well to be produced in a subject we cannot conceive capable of them, as well as in a subject we cannot conceive the motion of matter can any way operate upon? I say not this, that I would any way lessen the belief of the soul's immateriality: I am not here speaking of probability, but knowledge; and I think not only that it becomes the modesty of philosophy, not to pronounce magisterially, where we want that evidence that can produce knowledge; but also, that it is of use to us, to discern how far our knowledge does reach ... He that considers how hardly sensation is, in our thoughts, reconcilable to extended matter; or existence to anything that hath no extension at all, will confess, that he is very far from certainly knowing what his soul is. 'Tis a point, which seems to me, to be out of the reach of our knowledge: and he who will give himself leave to consider freely, and look into the dark and intricate part of each hypothesis, will scarce find his reason able to determine him fixedly for, or against the soul's materiality. Since on which side soever he views it, either as an unextended substance, or as a thinking extended matter; the difficulty to conceive either, will, whilst either alone is in his thoughts, still drive him to the contrary side. An unfair way which some men take with themselves: who, because of the unconceivableness of something they find in one, throw themselves violently into the contrary hypothesis, though altogether as unintelligible to an unbiassed understanding. This serves, not only to shew the weakness and scantiness of our knowledge, but the insignificant triumph of such sort of arguments, which, drawn from our own views, may satisfy us that we can find no certainty on one side of the question; but do not at all thereby help us to truth, by running into the opposite opinion, which, on examination, will be found clogg'd with equal difficulties. For what safety, what advantage to anyone is it, for the avoiding the seeming absurdities, and, to him, unsurmountable rubs he meets with in one opinion, to take refuge in the contrary, which is built on something altogether as inexplicable, and as far remote from his comprehension? 'Tis past controversy, that we have in us something that thinks, our very doubts about what it is, confirm the certainty of its being, though we must content ourselves in the ignorance of what kind of *being* it is: and 'tis in vain to go about to be sceptical in this, as it is unreasonable in most other cases to be positive against the being of any thing, because we cannot comprehend its nature. For I would fain know what substance exists that has not something in it, which manifestly baffles our understandings. (IV,iii.6)

Not surprisingly, Locke was accused of inconsistency by a critic, Stillingfleet, who found dualism embraced in the first passage (II.xxiii.5), but materialism allowed in the second. Locke responded that, in the first passage, 'spirit' simply means 'thinking substance', 'without considering what other modifications it has, as whether it has the modification of solidity or no'. In this sense there is no doubt that spirits exist, but we cannot know that they are not material, however improbable it may be. This defence seems feeble, if only because the issue with a dogmatic materialist such as Hobbes was whether the notion of an *immaterial* spirit makes sense. Hobbes did not, of course, deny that *material* thinking things exist. Locke's argument against the dogmatic materialist is that ordinary operations (and so the nature) of matter are just as mysterious to us as thought is, a point which some materialists (though not Hobbes, to whom nothing was mysterious) might be ready to take. What Locke needed, and presumably had in mind, was simply the obverse of the argument of the second passage (IV.iii.6) against dogmatic dualism. Thinking things are just as mysterious to us whether we take them to be material through and through or take them to be immaterial minds operating in combination with material bodies.

It might well seem, despite all kinds of whistling in the dark, that this remains the position even now – neither physics nor talk of souls has succeeded in explaining consciousness. 'Artificial intelligence' appears the giant step in that direction which some take it to be only if we are prepared to believe that some computers are conscious, and that the physiology of computers is not *importantly* different from the physiology of brains and nervous systems. Nevertheless, admirable and still relevant as Locke's warnings against dogmatic ways of thinking may be, substance-dualism is more deeply problematic than physicalism. Locke himself indicates the problems, in this and other passages. If immaterial spirits exist in space, the question arises not only how they interact with material things, but what spatial existence *is* for something not occupying space as bodies do. Indeed, what is it for something to exist in space which is not a part of physical nature, obedient to the laws of physics? What constitutes such a thing's existing in one place rather than another, if it is so unconnected with the rest of reality? The alternative, Cartesian view that spirits exist nowhere, extra-spatially (a view which Locke positively rejected), leaves us with the intractable problem of making sense of the individuality of spirits as 'substances' distinct from one another, according to some 'principle of individuation' other than the familiar one that distinct substantial things occupy different place-times. There are, then, good reasons for the current assumption that thinking is a physical process, quite apart from the progress that has been made in charting the functioning of the brain. Yet the general problem of integrating subjective experience with physics might well prompt the devout even today to assign the relation to 'the good pleasure of our maker' – which for Locke, it should be said, was simply to confess ignorance of created nature.

SPECIES

Locke's seemingly modest claim that our 'ideas of the particular sorts of substances' are formed of ideas of such qualities and powers 'as are by experience and observation of men's senses taken notice of to exist together' in fact carried a heavy and, it must be said, highly problematic theoretical load. It was a part of his uniquely thorough response to a challenge which faced any proponent of corpuscularianism, even one as cautious as Locke. That was the problem of what to say about species, since both the species of living things and the kinds of chemical substance played a central role in the Aristotelian and alchemical science which the New Philosophy was out to replace. The old model in biology was that of a hierarchical multiplicity of species and genera, each with its nature or form, a universal 'essence' to be identified and defined. On this theory, scientific definition of a kind divides a genus by the essential 'difference' of a lower genus or species, locating the kind in a natural hierarchy – in the 'tree' that rises from the category of substance, splits into living and non-living substances, each branch or genus splitting again and so on up to the ultimate twigs, the species. Such 'real' definition differs from mere 'nominal definition'. 'Real definition' identifies the explanatory essence from which flow other 'properties' of the species: that is, attributes common and natural to all its members. Hence their upright stance, possession of hands and capacity for speech and laughter allegedly flow from the defining rationality of human beings. 'Nominal definition', however, simply provides criteria for picking out members of the species. In chemistry, the nature of each substance was supposed to be determined by a proportion of elements – earth, air, fire and water – themselves definable by the qualitative 'opposites', hot and cold, wet and dry. Yet if corpuscularianism swept away the theory of forms and elements, how was it to explain the fairly striking appearance, at the level of ordinary observation, of a fixed hierarchy of related kinds under which every living creature falls? Or the seemingly rigid divisions between, say, distinct metals and acids, each found by experiment to interact with others and, in general, to respond to altered circumstances in dependable ways?

Locke was not the first of the New Philosophers to argue that nature is not such a cut-and-dried, orderly place as the Aristotelians assumed, but his argument is unique in its scope and its recourse to wider philosophical principles.

Here is his (biologically somewhat inaccurate) view of the 'Great Chain of Being':

> 12. ... That there should be more *species* of intelligent creatures above us, than there are of sensible and material below us, is probable to me from hence; that in all the visible corporeal world, we see no chasms, or gaps. All quite down from us, the descent is by easy steps, and a continued series of things, that in each remove, differ very little one from the other. There are fishes that have wings, and are not strangers to the airy region: and there are some birds, that are inhabitants of the water; whose blood is cold as fishes, and their flesh so like in taste, that the scrupulous are allow'd them on fish-days. There are animals so near of kin both to birds and beasts, that they are in the middle between both: amphibious animals link the terrestrial and aquatique together; seals live at land and at sea, and porpoises have the warm blood and entrails of a hog, not to mention what is confidently reported of mermaids, or sea-men. There are some brutes, that seem to have as much knowledge and reason, as some that are called men: and the animal and vegetable kingdoms, are so nearly join'd, that if you will take the lowest of one, and the highest of the other, there will scarce be perceived any great difference between them; and so on till we come to the lowest and the most inorganical parts of matter, we shall find everywhere, that the several species are linked together, and differ but in almost insensible degrees. (III.vi.12)

Not only is the orderly hierarchy of genera questioned here, but even divisions between species are put into doubt. In effect, Locke's natural world is composed of individuals linked by a network of criss-crossing resemblances, but liable to differ 'in almost insensible degrees'. Given such disorder and near-continuities, what are genera and species? Locke's answer is that they are human constructs, an answer which virtually follows from their being universal, since universality is a product of human practice: in particular, the practice of giving things general names on the basis of resemblance:

> 6. The next thing to be considered is, *how general words come to be made*. For since all things that exist are only particulars, how come we by general terms, or where find we those general natures they are supposed to stand for? Words become general, by being made the signs of general ideas: and ideas become general, by separating from them the circumstances of time, place, and any other ideas, that may determine them to this or that particular existence. By this way of abstraction they are made capable of representing more individuals than one; each of which, having in it a conformity to that abstract idea, is (as we call it) of that sort.

> 9. ... And he that thinks, general natures or notions, are anything else but such abstract and partial ideas of more complex ones, taken at first from particular existences, will, I fear, be at a loss where to find them. For let anyone reflect, and then tell me, wherein does his idea of *man* differ from that of *Peter*, and *Paul*; or his idea of *horse*, from that of *Bucephalus*, but in the leaving out something, that is peculiar to each individual; and

retaining so much of those particular complex ideas, of several particular existences, as they are found to agree in? Of the complex ideas, signified by the names *man*, and *horse*, leaving out but those particulars wherein they differ, and retaining only those wherein they agree, and of those making a new complex idea, and giving the name *animal* to it, one has a more general term, that comprehends, with man, several other creatures. Leave out of the idea of *animal*, sense and spontaneous motion, and the remaining complex idea, made up of the remaining simple ones of body, life and nourishment, becomes a more general one, under the more comprehensive term, *vivens* [living thing]. And not to dwell longer upon this particular, so evident in itself, by the same way the mind proceeds to *body*, *substance*, and at last to *being*, *thing*, and such universal terms, which stand for any of our ideas whatsoever. To conclude, this whole *mystery* of *genera* and *species*, which make such a noise in the Schools, and are, with justice, so little regarded out of them, is nothing else but abstract ideas, more or less comprehensive, with names annexed to them. (III.iii.6, 9)

This claim is supported by appeal to Locke's general theory of meaning, which accords with the whole form of his empiricist constructivism. The next passage is concerned with 'names' – Locke often just says 'words', despite his different account of words like 'is', 'but' and 'because'. The meanings of names, Locke holds, correspond to ways of conceiving of things: that is, to 'ideas'. Names are 'signs of internal conceptions', and ideas are signs of things.

2. ... *Words in their primary or immediate signification,* *stand for nothing, but the ideas in the mind of him that* *uses them,* how imperfectly soever, or carelessly those ideas are collected from the things, which they are supposed to represent. When a man speaks to another, it is, that he may be understood; and the end of speech is, that those sounds, as marks, may make known his ideas to the hearer. That then which words are the marks of, are the ideas of the speaker: nor can anyone apply them, as marks, immediately to anything else, but the ideas, that he himself hath: for this would be to make them signs of his own conceptions, and yet apply them to other ideas; which would be to make them signs, and not signs of his ideas at the same time; and so in effect, to have no signification at all. Words being voluntary signs, they cannot be voluntary signs imposed by him on things he knows not. That would be to make them signs of nothing, sounds without signification. A man cannot make his words the signs either of qualities in things, or of conceptions in the mind of another, whereof he has none of his own. Till he has some ideas of his own, he cannot suppose them to correspond with the conceptions of another man; nor can he use any signs for them: for thus they would be the signs of he knows not what, which is in truth to be the signs of nothing. But when he represents to himself other men's ideas, by some of his own, if he consent to give them the same names, that other men do, 'tis still to his own ideas; to ideas that he has, and not to ideas that he has not.

3. This is so necessary in the use of language, that in this

respect, the knowing and the ignorant; the learned, and unlearned, use the *words* they speak (with any meaning) all alike. They, *in every man's mouth, stand for the ideas he has*, and which he would express by them. (III.ii.2–3)

Consequently, words cannot be used, as Aristotelian theory implies, directly to name specific essences in the world, and the definition of a term can be nothing but the unpacking of a human conception, an 'abstract idea' formed on the basis of observed resemblances:

13. I would not here be thought to forget, much less to deny, that nature in the production of things, makes several of them alike: there is nothing more obvious, especially in the races of animals, and all things propagated by seed. But yet, I think, we may say, the *sorting* of them under names, *is the workmanship of the understanding, taking occasion from the similitude* it observes amongst them, to make abstract general ideas, and set them up in the mind, with names annexed to them, as patterns, or forms, (for in that sense the word *form* has a very proper signification,) to which, as particular things existing are found to agree, so they come to be of that species, have that denomination, or are put into that *classis*. For when we say, this is a *man*, that a *horse*; this *justice*, that *cruelty*; this a *watch*, that a *jack*; what do we else but rank things under different specific names, as agreeing to those abstract Ideas, of which we have made those names the signs? And what are the essences of those species, set out and marked by names, but those abstract Ideas in the mind; which are,

as it were, the bonds between particular things that exist and the names they are to be ranked under? (III.iii.13)

Locke's thesis commits him to two consequences, as questionable as they are radical. First, if meanings are so closely linked to 'ideas', it follows that people's meanings will differ as their knowledge differs. This is a consequence that Locke himself openly embraces: people with different knowledge and conceptions of 'the metal [they hear] called gold' will mean different things by the word 'gold'. Yet, whatever may be wrong with this semantic individualism, another consequence of his account of meaning is more to the present purpose. For his account implies that the general name of a chemical or living thing is tied to a complex appearance, much as the adjective 'white' is tied to a simple one. Yet, although it may in general be true that we rank things into kinds through their observable properties, we do so on the assumption that these properties are manifestations of an underlying nature which is what really determines membership of the kind in question. Leibniz pointed out, in direct criticism of Locke, that two substances might have the same appearance, although different natures. This may be thought, if not impossible, then undiscoverable, if the notion of 'the same appearance' is supposed to cover all possible observations. Yet, as Leibniz argued, it might well have been that, at some stage of human knowledge of gold, something not gold passed all known tests for gold. A new test and further observations might then have revealed the hidden difference.

Conversely, the same underlying nature might not be manifested in the same characteristic way in all cases.

Leibniz argued that the defining human capacity for rational thought might be present in an individual, although inhibited by some accidental abnormality. Accordingly, it can be held that whether two people mean the same thing by 'gold' or 'human' depends not on whether they have the same conception, or employ the same criteria for applying the term (the same 'nominal definition'), but simply on whether they use it for the same unknown or, rather, indirectly known underlying reality or nature: that is, in effect, whether they use it for the same instances or paradigms of the kind in question. What matters, that is to say, is that their different criteria map on to the same reality, and pick out individuals of the same real, natural kind.

Recent semantic theory has tended to confirm Leibniz's criticisms in important respects, but his defence of Aristotelian assumptions raised no issues unconsidered by Locke, who explicitly argued that the assumption that meaning can be determined by what is known only indirectly is an illusion. As we have seen, he allowed that we can in a sense refer to what is not directly known, and indeed do so through our ideas of secondary qualities and powers, but he argued that such reference is achieved only relatively to what *is* known and experienced. The illusion, for Locke, is to suppose that we can think of the unknown in some way not determined by what is known – which is what would be necessary for the meaning of names to be determined by hidden real essences:

> 19. ... For though in that called *gold*, one puts into his complex idea, what another leaves out; and *vice versa*: yet men do not usually think, that therefore the species

is changed: because they secretly in their minds refer that name, and suppose it annexed to a real immutable essence of a thing existing, on which those properties depend. He that adds to his complex idea of *gold*, that of fixedness or solubility in *aqua regia*, which he put not in it before, is not thought to have changed the species; but only to have a more perfect idea, by adding another simple idea, which is always in fact, joined with those other, of which his former complex idea consisted. But ... by this tacit reference to the real essence of that species of bodies, the word *gold* ... comes to have no signification at all, being put for somewhat, whereof we have no idea at all, and so can signify nothing at all, when the body itself is away. For however it may be thought all one; yet, if well considered, it will be found a quite different thing, to argue about *gold* in name, and about a parcel of the body itself, *v.g.* a piece of *leaf-gold* laid before us; though in discourse we are fain to substitute the name for the thing. (III.x.19)

This argument, tightly linking meaning with knowledge, does not, strictly speaking, rule out the possibility that there *is* a natural order of species and genera, but attempts to prove that we could not in any case hope to capture such an order by our classification, or to know if we had done so. For Locke, there is no possibility of identifying a species – that is, a specific essence – simply by reference to individual paradigms ('*v.g.* a piece of *leaf-gold* laid before us'), since talk of an essence (indeed, talk of 'leaf-gold') already assumes classification:

4. That *essence*, in the ordinary use of the word, relates to *sorts*, and that it is considered in particular beings, no

farther than as they are ranked into *sorts*, appears from hence: that take but away the abstract ideas, by which we sort individuals, and rank them under common names, and then the thought of anything *essential* to any of them, instantly vanishes: we have no notion of the one, without the other: which plainly shews their relation. 'Tis necessary for me to be as I am; GOD and nature has made me so: but there is nothing I have, is essential to me. An accident, or disease, may very much alter my colour, or shape; a fever, or fall, may take away my reason, or memory, or both; and an apoplexy leave neither sense, nor understanding, no nor life. Other creatures of my shape, may be made with more, and better, or fewer, and worse faculties than I have: and others may have reason, and sense, in a shape and body very different from mine. None of these are essential to the one, or the other, or to any individual whatsoever, till the mind refers it to some sort of *species* of things; and then presently, according to the abstract idea of that sort, something is found *essential*. Let any one examine his own thoughts, and he will find, that as soon as he supposes or speaks of *essential*, the consideration of some *species*, or the complex idea, signified by some general name, comes into mind: and 'tis in reference to that, that this or that quality is said to be *essential* …

5 … For I would ask any one, what is sufficient to make an *essential* difference in nature, between any two particular beings, without any regard had to some abstract idea, which is looked upon as the essence and standard of a *species*? All such patterns and standards, being quite laid

aside, particular beings, considered barely in themselves, will be found to have all their qualities equally *essential*; and everything, in each individual, will be *essential* to it, or, which is more true, nothing at all. For though it may be reasonable to ask, Whether obeying the magnet, be *essential* to *iron*? yet, I think, it is very improper and insignificant to ask, Whether it be *essential* to the particular parcel of matter I cut my pen with, without considering it under the name *iron*, or as being of a certain *species*? And if, as has been said, our abstract ideas, which have names annexed to them, are the boundaries of *species*, nothing can be *essential* but what is contained in those ideas. (III.vi.4–5)

This argument about classification is quite general, but it is largely motivated by its consonance with Locke's belief as to what most probably lies behind things' observable properties: namely, quasi-mechanical structures temporarily surviving within the flux of corpuscles. For these are so different from Aristotelian universal essences that they seem to Locke to be as incapable of supplying boundaries between species as, without human decision, the observable properties themselves. Given a classification, we can talk of the 'real constitutions' of species – of the structures which lie behind the observable properties figuring in our definitions – but 'real constitutions' of individuals taken simply as such are in continual flux. Locke makes the point by distinguishing between 'real essences' and 'nominal essences', echoing the Aristotelian distinction between real and nominal definitions. His argument is dialectical, first envisaging individual 'real essences', and then moving to the view that, since *'essence ... relates to a sort'*, meaningful talk of a 'real essence' is always relative to a nominal essence.

19. ... All things, that exist, besides their Author, are all liable to change; especially those things we are acquainted with, and have ranked into bands, under distinct names or ensigns. Thus that, which was grass today, is tomorrow the flesh of a sheep; and within **few** days after, becomes part of a man: in all which, and the like changes, 'tis evident, their real *essence*, i.e. that constitution, whereon the properties of these several things depended, is destroy'd, and perishes with them. But *essences* being taken for ideas, established in the mind, with names annexed to them, they are supposed to remain steadily the same, whatever mutations the particular substances are liable to ... By this means the *essence* of a *species* rests safe and entire, without the existence of so much as one individual of that kind. (III.iii.19)

6. 'Tis true, I have often mentioned a *real essence*, distinct in substances, from those abstract ideas of them, which I call their *nominal essence*. By this *real essence*, I mean, that real constitution of any thing, which is the foundation of all those properties, that are combined in, and are constantly found to co-exist with the *nominal essence*; that particular constitution, which every thing has within itself, without any relation to anything without it. But *essence*, even in this sense, *relates to a sort,* and supposes a *species*: for being that real constitution, on which the properties depend, it necessarily supposes a sort of things, properties belonging only to *species*, and not to

individuals; *v.g.* supposing the nominal essence of *gold*, to be body of such a peculiar colour and weight, with malleability and fusibility, the real essence is that constitution of the parts of matter, on which these qualities, and their union, depend; and is also the foundation of its solubility in *aqua regia*, and other properties accompanying that complex Idea. Here are *essences* and *properties*, but all upon supposition of a sort, or general abstract idea, which is considered as immutable: but there is no individual parcel of matter, to which any of these qualities are so annexed, as to be *essential* to it, or inseparable from it ... Indeed, as to the *real essences* of substances, we only suppose their being, without precisely knowing what they are: but that which annexes them still to the *species*, is the nominal essence of which they are the supposed foundation and cause. (III.vi.6)

Having rejected the ideal of a 'natural system' based on real essences, Locke develops his classic, influential conception of good practical classification: we should draw boundaries wherever seems most useful for collecting the results of careful observation and experiment, but never lose sight of the importance of general agreement, without which language itself tends to lose its point. The argument, like most of these discussed in this book, has more complexities and implications than can be explored here. And, like all the arguments discussed, it is a part of Locke's central enterprise of charting the relation between experience and theory. The effects of that enterprise, and of Locke's insights and errors, are still with us, often so much a part of our intellectual heritage as to escape notice.